Sam's Christmas Angel

ISBN: 0-8862-0015-2

Design: Diane Stevenson of Snap-Haus Graphics

Sam's
Christmas Angel

Sheila Black
Illustrated by Paul Selwyn

Ariel Books·Andrews and McMeel·Kansas City

Sam glanced out the window at the blue starry sky and the swaying palm trees. It was Christmas Eve. His parents were upstairs wrapping presents. Sam was in the living room with his grandmother, who had just come to live with them. Sam watched as Grandma shook the snowdome she was holding in her hand. Snowflakes twirled down around the little angel inside. Sam smiled. "Tell me again about Christmas in Vermont, Grandma," he said. "Did you always have snow?"

Grandma smiled too. "Oh, my yes. Snow, snow, and more snow. We always went sledding on Christmas Eve. And we always had a big snowball fight Christmas morning even though it drove our mother crazy!" She jiggled the snowdome again. "My little angel reminds me of all those happy white Christmases."

"I wish it would snow here," said Sam, "so you and I could have a white Christmas together." He remembered that Grandma once told him that she used to make wishes on the little angel in the snowdome when she was a girl. "Maybe we could ask the angel to bring us snow."

"Oh, Sam," Grandma sighed, "snow in Florida is rarer than a blue moon. I doubt even a real angel could make it snow. But here-you can have my angel snowdome, Sam. That way you can watch it snow as often as you like."

"Thanks, Grandma." Sam stuck the snowdome in the pocket of his pajamas.

Sam's mother kissed him good night and turned out the light. Sam glanced at the snowdome on his night table. In the moonlight it looked as if the angel inside were smiling at him. "I wish you could make it snow for Christmas," Sam whispered to her. "It would make Grandma so happy!" The angel didn't say anything. Sam closed his eyes. He didn't think he could sleep because it was Christmas Eve, and Sam never felt sleepy on Christmas Eve. But in no time at all he was fast asleep.

"Sam! Sam! Wake up!"

"Go away," Sam mumbled, opening one eye. Then he sat up. Hovering over him was the angel from the snowdome. Only now she was big-as big as he was! "I can't believe it," Sam gasped. "You're real! But what are you doing here?" The angel laughed, filling the room with a happy sound like Christmas bells.

"That's a surprise," she said, with a grin. "Come on, we have a lot to do before morning." And she stretched out her hand to Sam.

"I must be dreaming," Sam mumbled, as he followed the angel out the open window. "But it's the greatest dream I've ever had." He felt the fresh night air ripple across his cheeks. "Maybe this isn't a dream," he thought. He and the angel were flying over the big pond at the bottom of his backyard. Sam could hear frogs croaking and see baby alligators sleeping on the banks.

"Ooops," the angel said, as she pulled Sam out of the path of a coconut tree. "We better fly a little higher."

Soon they were gliding along the seashore. A cold wind was blowing and Sam was glad he was wearing his warmest pajamas. He could see seabirds asleep in their nests on the rocks far below and ships decorated with sparkling Christmas lights. "Where are we going?" he asked the angel.

Her eyes twinkled. "I told you—it's a surprise." Suddenly, she tugged at his sleeve. "Duck!" she shouted.

Sam ducked, then looked up just in time to see a shiny silver sleigh whiz past. The sleigh was pulled by eight glossy brown reindeer, and holding the reins was a plump, white-haired old man in a bright red suit. "Merry Christmas! Ho! Ho! Ho!" the old man called.

"But that's~" Sam was so excited he could hardly speak.

"Yes," the angel nodded, "so it is. And he's in just as much of a hurry to go south as we are to go north."

"North?" Sam repeated. He looked down. Instead of palm trees and flowers, he saw high rocky mountains and dark, dense forests. The air smelled different too-of frost and pine. Sam shivered. "I hope we don't go too much farther north," he thought, "I'm not dressed for this weather." And for a moment, he wished he were back in his own bed. But when the angel smiled at him, Sam felt warm and happy again. Suddenly something landed on his nose-something cold and soft. Sam looked up-"Snow!" he shouted in delight. Big beautiful white flakes were softly drifting down all around him. Sam caught one in his hand. "It's snowing!" The angel laughed. This time her laughter sounded not like bells, but like people singing a joyous song with all their hearts.

"Yes," she said. "It's snowing. And we're almost there."

"Almost where?" Sam asked.

"Almost to the North Pole, of course," replied the angel. "It's the best place I know to meet a snowstorm."

"Meet a snowstorm?" Sam cried. "What do you mean?"

The angel smiled. "I thought you wanted a white Christmas for your grandmother?"

"I did. I mean, I do, but~"

"Well, if you want a white Christmas," the angel interrupted, "you have to fetch a snowstorm. It's as simple as that." And she tugged Sam even higher into the sky.

Looking down, Sam saw that they were at the very top of the world, where the snow comes from. He could see glittering icebergs and frolicking polar bears. Looking up, he saw cold, white clouds gathering.

"Get ready," said the angel. And they jumped up onto the largest cloud of all.

Sam saw snowflakes falling all around. Snowflakes of all sizes in patterns more lovely than he could ever have imagined. "Hold on tight," the angel whispered. "Once these storms get going, they move awfully fast." Sam squeezed the angel's hand. The next thing he knew, he was whirling and swirling along in a glimmering cloud of snowflakes.

Sam's eyelids were starting to feel very heavy. "I bet it's way past my bedtime," he thought. Aloud he said, "I can't believe we're really going to have a white Christmas. Grandma will be so surprised!" He looked at the angel. "Do you always make kids' Christmas wishes come true?"

The angel shook her head. "Not always."

"Then why did you make my wish come true?"

"Because you wanted to make someone happy," the angel replied, as Sam's eyes slowly drifted shut. "You see, Sam, that's a very important lesson of Christmas: no matter how nice it is to get, it's even nicer to give." Then Sam felt himself falling, just like a spinning snowflake, and he landed with a thump back in his very own bed.

"Wake up, sleepyhead. It's Christmas!" Sam opened his eyes. His mother, father, and grandmother were standing by his bed. "Don't you want to come down and see your presents?"

"Yes!" Sam sat up. Then he looked out the window. The sky was cloudy and blowy looking, but there was no snow anywhere. Splat! A fat raindrop hit the window. Sam's face fell. "I guess it was only a dream," he muttered. He picked up the little angel, put her back in his pajama pocket, and followed the others downstairs.

When Sam was halfway down the stairs, his mother shouted, "Come here, everyone! Quick!" Sam blinked. The front door stood wide open. His mother, father, and grandmother had run outside.

"Wait for me!" Sam raced down the stairs and out the door. "Snow!" he cried. Hundreds of sparkly, shimmery snowflakes were twirling down out of the sky, falling gently on the palm trees, the frogs, and even the baby alligators.

"It's a white Christmas," said Sam's father. "I can't believe it."

"It's a miracle," said Sam's mother.

"It's Sam's Christmas wish," said Grandma, so softly that only Sam could hear her. He looked at his grandmother and smiled. Grandma smiled too—the widest smile Sam had ever seen.

"I guess sometimes wishes really do come true," Grandma said, and gave Sam a hug. "Thanks, Sam, and Merry Christmas."

"Merry Christmas, Grandma." Sam reached in to his pocket, pulled out the snowdome, and peered at the little angel inside. He wasn't absolutely sure, but he thought she was winking at him.